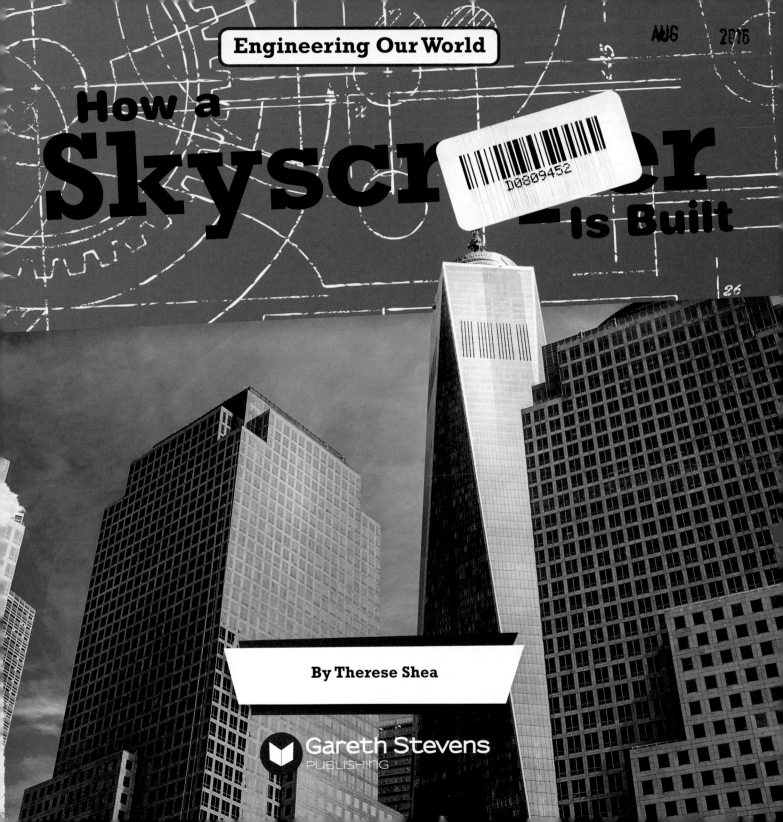

Engineering Our World

AUG 2016

How a Skyscraper Is Built

By Therese Shea

Gareth Stevens
PUBLISHING

Please visit our website, www.garethstevens.com. For a free color catalog of all our high-quality books, call toll free 1-800-542-2595 or fax 1-877-542-2596.

Library of Congress Cataloging-in-Publication Data

Shea, Therese, author.
 How a skyscraper is built / Therese Shea.
     pages cm. — (Engineering our world)
 Includes index.
 ISBN 978-1-4824-3935-9 (pbk.)
 ISBN 978-1-4824-3936-6 (6 pack)
 ISBN 978-1-4824-3937-3 (library binding)
 1. Skyscrapers—Design and construction—Juvenile literature. I. Title.
 TH1615.S54 2016
 720.483—dc23

                                2015031494

First Edition

Published in 2016 by
Gareth Stevens Publishing
111 East 14th Street, Suite 349
New York, NY 10003

Copyright © 2016 Gareth Stevens Publishing

Designer: Samantha DeMartin
Editor: Ryan Nagelhout

Photo credits: Cover, p. 1 VOJTa Herout/Shutterstock.com; caption box stoonn/Shutterstock.com; background Jason Winter/Shutterstock.com; p. 5 (main) dibrova/Shutterstock.com; p. 5 (inset) Goodluz/Shutterstock.com; p. 7 rootstock/Shutterstock.com; p. 9 Jozef Sowa/Shutterstock.com; p. 11 AlexKZ/Shutterstock.com; p. 13 canadastock/Shutterstock.com; p. 15 Paul Matthew Photography/Shutterstock.com; p. 17 (inset) STAN HONDA/AFP/Getty Images; p. 17 (main) Naufal MQ/Moment/Getty Images; p. 19 (inset) View Pictures/Universal Images Group/Getty Images; p. 19 (main) zohaib anjum/Shutterstock.com; p. 20 (newspaper) RTimages/Shutterstock.com; p. 20 (scissors) Vladvm/Shutterstock.com; p. 20 (tape) Sean MacD/Shutterstock.com; p. 21 (child) Blaj Gabriel/Shutterstock.com; p. 21 (fan) a_v_d/Shutterstock.com.

Printed in the United States of America

CPSIA compliance information: Batch #CW16GS: For further information contact Gareth Stevens, New York, New York at 1-800-542-2595.

Contents

Words in the glossary appear in **bold** type the first time they are used in the text.

Look Up!

Some people say a skyscraper is any building 20 stories or taller. Others say 50 stories or taller. Still others think a skyscraper is any building that makes someone stop to look up at its height. Did you ever wonder how such a building is made?

Architects usually create the **design** of a skyscraper. However, it's up to engineers to plan and oversee the construction of the building. They make certain the building can stand up to forces such as **gravity** and strong winds.

Building Blocks

Engineers are people who use science and math to solve problems with products, structures, or processes. Different kinds of engineers, including structural engineers and earthquake engineers, may work together to build a skyscraper.

There isn't much room for new buildings in crowded cities. Building up means more space for working and living.

Super Steel

Have you ever had to make a model of something for school? Whether it was a dinosaur, a volcano, or something else, you started out with certain **materials** you knew you'd need. Two key materials used in skyscraper construction today are steel and reinforced concrete.

Steel is an **alloy** of iron and carbon. Reinforced concrete is a mix of cement, water, and gravel or sand that's poured onto steel rods. Both materials give skyscrapers the great strength they need to stay upright.

Building Blocks

Other materials that may be used in skyscrapers include glass, aluminum, stainless steel, granite, marble, and limestone.

This photo shows steel rods before and after they're covered with concrete to make a reinforced concrete **column**.

A Firm Foundation

All skyscrapers must have a strong **foundation**. To create a foundation, a deep pit is dug down to **bedrock**. Holes are then blasted in the bedrock, and steel or reinforced concrete support columns are placed in them.

If the bedrock is too deep to reach by digging, columns called piles are driven into the soil until they're fixed in the bedrock. In another method, **shafts** are drilled into the soil and bedrock, and steel rods are placed in them. The shafts are then filled with concrete.

Building Blocks

Vertical columns in a skyscraper's foundation often sit on a spread footing. This means the bottom of the column is wider, allowing it to bear more weight.

If you've ever built a tower of blocks, you know that it falls over when it gets too tall. That's why a skyscraper needs a strong foundation.

The Superstructure

Gravity is always pulling down on a skyscraper. An engineer plans a skyscraper so that the foundation and many beams share its great weight.

Just like your body needs a bony frame, or skeleton, to hold you up, a skyscraper needs a steel skeleton to support its weight. Metal beams are fixed to each other to form vertical and **horizontal** columns. There might be **diagonal** beams as well. This skeleton is called the superstructure.

Building Blocks

Many skyscrapers have a concrete core, or center, that bears weight.

It would be impossible to build skyscrapers without huge cranes. Cranes lift heavy materials into place.

11

Inside and Out

Many skyscrapers seem to be made of glass, but they aren't really. Their superstructures are doing the hard work of holding the buildings up, so their outside walls can be made of anything, including glass or metal.

As a skyscraper's superstructure is built higher and higher, crews begin to work to lay floors and finish construction on lower stories. This work includes adding electrical wires, plumbing, inner walls, bathrooms, lighting, and heating and cooling.

Building Blocks

Because it would be hard for people on upper floors to escape in a fire, fireproof materials and sprinkler systems are important in skyscraper construction to keep the building and people inside safe.

Engineers may also be involved in planning and setting up electrical and mechanical systems in skyscrapers.

Going Up!

Can you imagine walking into a skyscraper and climbing 50 flights of stairs? There wouldn't be skyscrapers if there weren't elevators! Most skyscrapers feature an elevator shaft in the middle of the building, but some elevators are on an outside wall.

The more stories a building is, the more people occupy it. That means more elevators are needed. Engineers use math to figure out how many elevators are needed to keep people moving up and down. They also need to figure out how more elevators will affect the structure of the building.

Building Blocks

In 1956, famous architect Frank Lloyd Wright said he was designing a skyscraper for 100,000 workers that would be 1 mile (1.6 km) tall. It was never built, but can you imagine how many elevators would be needed?

The first passenger elevator was placed in a building in New York City in 1857. Other elevators are used to move objects up and down quickly.

The Power of Wind

Another force an engineer needs to consider when building skyscrapers is wind. Tall buildings may move back and forth in the wind. This doesn't feel safe to the people inside, even if the building is strong enough to hold up in the wind. So, there are certain ways of constructing a skyscraper that can help.

In shorter skyscrapers, tightened connections between horizontal and vertical beams can keep the building from moving in the wind. Taller skyscrapers use stronger cores to keep the building from swaying. Some buildings have more than one core, strengthened by steel.

Building Blocks

The Citigroup Center in New York City uses a concrete weight to shift the weight of the building from side to side to keep from moving in the wind. A computer measures the wind and moves the weight.

Citigroup Center

A breeze on the ground can be a powerful wind at the top of a skyscraper. A model of a skyscraper may be tested in a special wind tunnel to make sure it's steady before it's built.

Superior Skyscrapers

Over the years, engineers have found ways to make skyscrapers taller and taller. Currently, the tallest building in the world is the Burj Khalifa in the city of Dubai in the United Arab Emirates. It's 2,716.5 feet (828 m) tall. Its special shape supports its weight as well as makes winds travel around it rather than push against it.

Another skyscraper is under construction that's planned to be 3,281 feet (1,000 m) tall. The Kingdom Tower in Jeddah, Saudia Arabia, is expected to be finished by 2018. It will have 57 elevators in all!

Building Blocks

Some buildings aren't just tall, they're unusual in other ways. In Bangkok, Thailand, a building was constructed to look like a robot.

Burj Khalifa holds many records, including having the longest-traveling elevator in the world.

The Robot Building

Make Your Own Skyscraper

Now that you know how a skyscraper is built, let's use some newspaper to make your own superstructure!

What You Need:

- fan

- newspaper

- scissors

- tape

How To:

1. roll newspaper to make tube

2. tape tube vertically

3. roll more paper to make foundation tubes

4. secure foundation to ground

5. tape foundation tubes to vertical tube

6. test structure with fan

7. make foundation stronger if it falls over

Glossary

alloy: matter made of two or more metals, or a metal and a nonmetal, melted together

architect: a person who designs a building

bedrock: the solid rock that lies under the surface of the ground

column: a long, tall piece of matter that holds something up

design: the pattern or shape of something. Also, to create the pattern or shape of something.

diagonal: slanting from one side to another

foundation: a structure, usually made of stone or concrete, that supports a building from underneath

gravity: the force that pulls objects toward Earth's center

horizontal: level with the line that seems to form where the earth meets the sky

material: something used to make something else

shaft: a vertical opening or passage through something

For More Information

Books

Brasch, Nicolas. *Triumphs of Engineering*. New York, NY: PowerKids Press, 2013.

Encarnacion, Elizabeth. *Skyscrapers*. Laguna Hills, CA: QEB Publishing, 2007.

Hurley, Michael. *The World's Most Amazing Skyscrapers*. Chicago, IL: Raintree, 2012.

Websites

Building Big: Skyscrapers
pbs.org/wgbh/buildingbig/skyscraper/
Read about famous skyscrapers on this website.

Building Facts
www.sciencekids.co.nz/sciencefacts/engineering/buildings.html
Check out some more facts about skyscrapers and other buildings.

Index